LEARN ABOUT

FLIGHT

PETER MELLETT

LORENZ BOOKS
NEW YORK • LONDON • SYDNEY • BATH

This edition first published in 1997 by Lorenz Books
27 West 20th Street, New York, NY 10011

LORENZ BOOKS are available for bulk purchase
for sales promotion and for premium use. For details,
write or call the sales director: Lorenz Books,
27 West 20th Street, New York, NY 10011;
(800) 354-9657

Lorenz Books is an imprint of
Anness Publishing Limited

TB   VB

ISBN 1-85967-311-2

Publisher: Joanna Lorenz
Managing Editor, Children's Books: Sue Grabham
Editor: Charlotte Evans
Consultant: Chris Oxlade
Photographer: John Freeman
Stylists: Marion Elliot and Melanie Williams
Designer: Caroline Grimshaw
Picture Researcher: Liz Eddison
Illustrator: Dave Bowyer

Printed and bound in China

1 3 5 7 9 10 8 6 4 2

The Publishers would like to thank the following children, and their
parents, for modeling in this book—Emily Askew, Sara Barnes,
Maria Bloodworth, David Callega, Aaron Dumetz, Laurence de Freitas,
Alistair Fulton, Anton Goldbourne, Sasha Howarth, Jon Leming,
Jessica Moxley, Ifunanya Obi, Emily Preddie, Elen Rhys,
Nicola Twiner and Joe Westbrook.

FLIGHT

CONTENTS

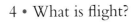

WHAT IS FLIGHT?

Think of flight and you think birds and insects, paper planes and airplanes, bullets and footballs. All of these things can move swiftly through the air, but are they all really flying? To answer this question, imagine you are launching a paper plane into the air. It glides away from you and finally lands back on the ground. Now throw a ball in exactly the same way. It hits the ground much sooner than the paper plane. We say that the paper plane was flying, but the ball was not. This is because bullets, footballs, stones and arrows are all projectiles. They do not really fly because they have nothing to keep them up in the air. Birds, aircraft, rockets and balloons *do* fly—they stay off the ground longer than something that is simply thrown.

Animal power
Birds, insects and bats all have wings. These animals use their wings to hold themselves up in the air and move along. Muscles provide power for takeoff.

Balloons
This balloon is filled with a gas called *helium*. It is lighter than air so the balloon floats upward, just like a cork floats upward in water. This is how hot-air balloons and airships are able to fly. Before airplanes and rockets were invented, the only way people could make a sustained flight was in a structure lighter than air, such as a balloon.

Spaceflight
The space shuttle is launched into space by booster rockets. It uses its own rocket engines to reach an orbit about 180 miles above the earth. Earth's force of gravity acts like a tether, keeping the shuttle in orbit, while the shuttle's speed prevents it from falling back to the ground.

Airplanes

Airplanes have wings like birds to hold them up in the air, but they also have engines. Engine power is needed to push airplanes through the air and provide enough power to help them take off from the ground.

Tether

Flying a kite

A kite is lifted into the air by a blowing wind. A long string, called a *tether*, holds the kite at an angle to the wind. The rushing air pushes against the kite, pushing it upward and keeping it in the air. If the wind drops or the tether breaks, the kite will fall back to the ground.

Gliders

Gliders have no engines, so they have to be towed into the air by small airplanes or by machines on the ground. On release, their wings hold them up in the air as they glide slowly back to the ground in a gentle spiral. The pilot controls the glider's flight by searching for rising air currents and by altering the shape of the glider's wings.

WINGS AND LIFT

FLAP your arms up and down like a bird—you cannot take off because you are not designed to fly. You are the wrong shape and your muscles are not strong enough. Birds have wings and powerful muscles that enable them to fly. Flapping provides a force called *thrust*, which moves a bird forward through the air. A bird's wings are a special shape, called an airfoil. In an *airfoil*, the top side is more curved than the underneath. This shape helps to keep a bird up in the air, even when its wings are not flapping. When an airfoil wing moves through the air, it creates an upward push. This push is a force called *lift*. It works in opposition to the weight of the object, which because of gravity, pulls the object down toward the ground. There are many different shapes and sizes of birds, gliders and airplanes, but they all have airfoil wings.

Blowing across a sheet of paper reduces the pressure of the air above the paper. The stronger pressure beneath lifts the paper up.

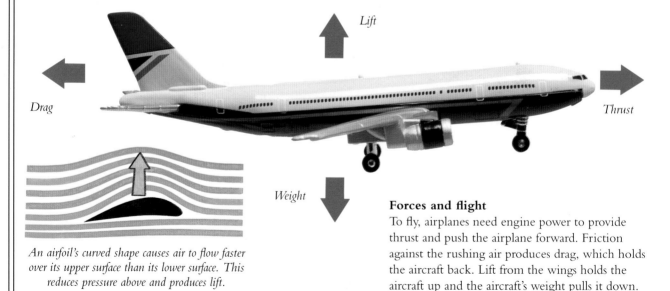

Lift

Drag

Thrust

Weight

An airfoil's curved shape causes air to flow faster over its upper surface than its lower surface. This reduces pressure above and produces lift.

Forces and flight
To fly, airplanes need engine power to provide thrust and push the airplane forward. Friction against the rushing air produces drag, which holds the aircraft back. Lift from the wings holds the aircraft up and the aircraft's weight pulls it down.

Wings and soaring

This bird is soaring through the air without flapping its wings. As its wings slice through the air, the force of lift pushes up on them. The faster the bird's speed, the greater the lift. It is able to glide like this for many hours.

- The latest jumbo jet, the Boeing 747-400, weighs about 385 tons at takeoff. A third of this weight is fuel, which is stored in its wings. It has a wingspan of 180 feet.

- Most helicopters have from three to six rotor blades. The blades are more than 30 feet long, but only about 1½ feet wide.

- The speed of a jumbo jet reaches almost 180 miles per hour at takeoff.

- Half the weight of a pigeon is taken up by the flight muscles needed to flap its wings.

- A boomerang is a bent airfoil wing. The oldest boomerang is 20,000 years old and was found in a cave in Poland.

Helicopters

Airplanes have wings that do not move. The planes must rush through the air so that their wings work. Helicopters have long thin airfoil wings called *rotor blades*. Powerful engines whirl the blades around so that the blades produce lift. Helicopters can hover, or fly forward, backward and sideways, as well as straight up and down.

Taking off

Most airplanes need long runways to take off. They speed along, getting faster and faster, until the lift pushing up is greater than the weight pulling down, allowing them to leave the ground.

MAKE AN AIRFOIL

Birds, gliders and airplanes all have wings. Their wings can be all sorts of different shapes and sizes, but they all have the same airfoil design. This means that the top side of the wing is more curved than the underneath. From a tiny sparrow to a huge airliner, the airfoil shape provides lift when air moves over it. Air flows faster over the curved upper surface than the flatter, lower surface. This reduces the air pressure above the wing and allows the stronger air pressure underneath to lift it up.

You can make and test a model airfoil by following the instructions for these projects. They will show you how moving air lifts wings upward. In the first project, a frisbee is a circular airfoil shaped like a dish. Just like a straight wing, air flows faster over its top surface than its underneath. The frisbee spins as it flies. This motion helps to steady it.

M A T E R I A L S

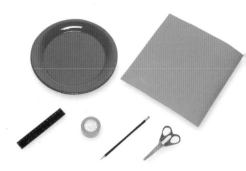

You will need:
a large plate, thick cardboard, pencil, scissors, ruler, tape.

Make a frisbee

1 Place the plate face down on the cardboard and draw around it with a pencil. Cut out the circle. Draw slots about 1 inch deep around the edge and cut along these, as well.

2 The cut slots around the edge will make tabs. Bend the tabs down slightly. Overlap them a little and stick them together with small pieces of tape.

3 Fly your frisbee outside, away from people. Hold it at the front and spin it away from you and up.

Make an airfoil

1 Cut out a rectangle of paper 6 inches wide and 8 inches long. Draw a line down the middle.

2 Fold the paper over. Use tape to stick the top edge about ½ inch away from the bottom edge.

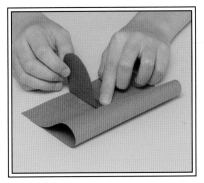

3 Cut out and stick on a small fin near the rear edge of your wing. This will keep the wing facing into the airflow when you test it.

MATERIALS

You will need: paper, pencil, ruler, scissors, tape, glue, plastic drinking straw, thick cotton yarn.

4 With a sharp pencil, poke a hole through the top and bottom of your wing, near the front edge. Push a straw through the holes and glue it in place in the middle.

5 Cut a 3-foot-long piece of thick cotton yarn and thread it through the straw. Make sure the yarn can slide easily through the straw and does not catch.

Hold the yarn tight and blow air from a fan or hair dryer over the wing. Watch it take off! Do you know how this happens?

AIR RESISTANCE

WHEN you are swimming, you have to push your way through the water. As you swim, the water is resisting you and slowing you down. In the same way, things that fly have to push their way through the air. Air clings to their surfaces as they rush through it. The result is a backward pull called *drag*, or *air resistance*, which works against the direction of flight. Drag is the force that slows down anything that is flying through the air. Drag depends on shape. Fat, lumpy shapes with sharp edges create a lot of drag. They disturb the air and make it swirl around as they move along. Sleek, streamlined shapes have low drag and can fly the fastest. They hardly disturb the air as they cut smoothly through it. For any shape, increasing the speed increases the drag. Double the speed creates four times the amount of drag. The result is that drag limits how fast anything can fly.

Parachutes fall slowly because they trap air underneath. They are designed to have very high drag.

Angle of attack

When an aircraft is in flight, the angle its wings make to the airflow is called the angle of attack. If the angle of attack is increased, the amount of lift also increases.

If the angle of attack becomes too great, lift drops suddenly. The smooth flow of air over the wing is broken, creating turbulence, increasing drag and reducing lift.

Turbulence

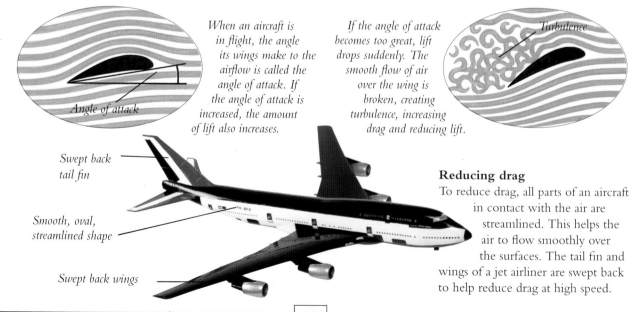

Swept back tail fin

Smooth, oval, streamlined shape

Swept back wings

Reducing drag
To reduce drag, all parts of an aircraft in contact with the air are streamlined. This helps the air to flow smoothly over the surfaces. The tail fin and wings of a jet airliner are swept back to help reduce drag at high speed.

Birds must slow down before they land. This owl has tipped up its wings so that the undersides face forward. It has also lowered and spread out its tail feathers to act as a brake. Drag increases suddenly, lift decreases and the bird drops to its landing place.

The Concorde can fly at a speed of over 1,200 miles per hour. Its wings are swept back to reduce drag. If its wings stuck straight out they would be ripped off at this speed.

The Lockheed SR-71 lands at 210 miles per hour. A parachute helps it slow down, as ordinary brakes on its wheels would take too long.

Coming in to land, an airliner uses flaps on its wings to increase lift at low speeds. During flight, these flaps are retracted to reduce drag.

STREAMLINING AND SHAPE

THINK of a sleek canoe moving through water. Its streamlined shape makes hardly any ripples. Streamlined shapes also move easily through air. We say that they have low *drag*. Drag is also called *air resistance*. It is the force that works against the forward motion of flight. Drag is affected by shape. Angular shapes have more drag than rounded ones. Design and test your own streamlined shapes, or make a model parachute and find out how its shape is designed to have high drag so it falls slowly.

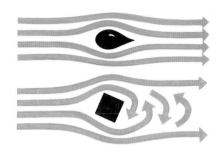

Air flows in gentle curves around the streamlined shape (top). Angles or sharp edges break up the flow and increase drag.

Shape race

Make different shapes (*as shown at right*) from balls of modeling clay all the same size. Race your shapes in water—the most streamlined shape should reach the bottom first.

Star shape   *Square shape*   *Teardrop shape*

How much of a splash would you make diving into a pool? This diver's streamlined shape will help her cut cleanly through the water to dive deep down.

MATERIALS

You will need:
felt-tip pen, a large plate,
thin fabric, scissors, needle,
cotton thread, tape,
plastic thread spool.

Make a parachute

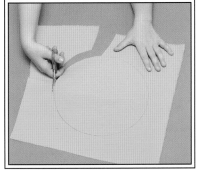

1 Use the felt-tip pen to draw around the plate on the fabric. Carefully cut out the circle to make the parachute's canopy.

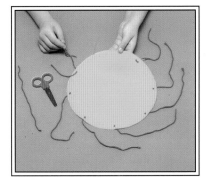

2 Make about 8 equally spaced marks around the edge of the circle. Use a needle to sew on a 12-inch-long piece of cotton thread at each point you have marked.

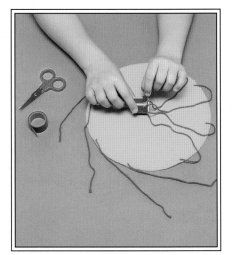

3 Tape the free end of each thread to the spool. Be sure to use a plastic spool, because a wooden one will be too heavy for your parachute.

4 Let your parachute go from as high up as possible. As it falls, the canopy will open and fill with air. The larger the canopy, the slower the parachute will fall.

GLIDING AND SOARING

A glider is towed into the air attached to a cable. Its long, thin wings give maximum lift and minimum drag for their size. If a glider flies level in still air, drag forces slow it down and the wings lose their lift. So, to keep up speed, a glider flies on a gradual downward slope.

WATCH a small bird as it flies. It flaps its wings very fast almost the whole time. Large birds, however, often glide with their large wings stretched out flat and still. They can do this because their wings create enough lift to keep them up in the air without flapping. Soaring birds, such as albatrosses and condors, fly for hours, hardly moving their wings at all. They gain height by using rising air currents over the land and sea.

Gliders are aircraft that do not have engines. They have wings like those of soaring birds. They are pulled along by small aircraft or by machines on the ground, until the lift generated by their wings keeps them airborne. Glider pilots seek out rising air currents, called *thermals*, to lift their aircraft.

Going up

Pilots look for thermals (rising air currents) to gain height. Thermals happen where the wind is forced upward by cliffs or hillsides, or where the air is heated by the ground. Hot air rises because it is pushed up by the cold air around it. The glider circles inside the thermal, steadily gaining height as the rising air carries it up. At the top of the thermal the effect is weaker, so the pilot stops circling and flies straight on.

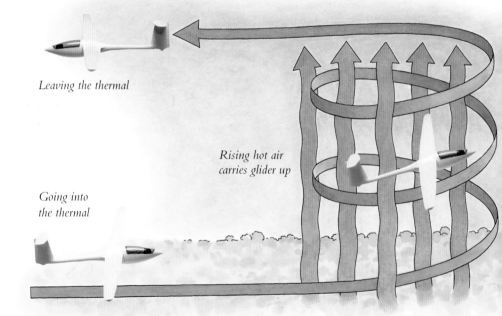

Leaving the thermal

Rising hot air carries glider up

Going into the thermal

Paraglider

A paraglider's wing shape is made by air blowing into pockets on its leading edge. The pilot steers from side to side and can ride up thermals.

Albatrosses have long narrow wings. This wing shape helps them to glide for enormous distances on air currents blowing over the open ocean. At over 9 feet long, albatrosses have the longest wingspan of any bird.

This picture shows the inside of a glider's cockpit, high above ground. The left-hand dial gives forward air speed. The middle dial shows the rate of climb or descent (how fast the glider is going up or down). The last dial on the right shows the glider's altitude, or height above ground.

Hang glider

Made from strong, thin material stretched over a framework of aluminum poles, a hang glider is very light. The material on the hang glider's wing is stretched into an airfoil shape to produce lift. To steer the hang glider, the pilot moves a control bar forward to climb and backward to dive.

KITES AND SAILS

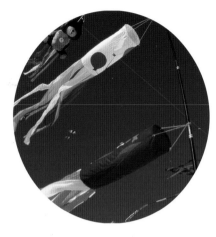

Have you ever been blown over by the wind? Wind is moving air—it pushes against anything standing in its path. You can fly a kite because it is held up in the air by the force of the wind pushing against it. A string, called a *tether*, connects the kite to the ground and holds it at the correct angle to the wind. You can feel tension along the tether as it pulls on your hand. The tension is the result of the wind blowing against the kite and lifting it up. If the tether broke, the kite would no longer be held at the correct angle and it would fall to the ground. When there is no wind, a kite can still be made to fly by pulling it through the air.

Lift
Air blowing into the kite creates lift.

Flying a kite
What makes a kite fly? Wind is deflected downward when it blows against a kite. This pushes the kite upward and creates lift and drag. The tether keeps the kite at an angle to the wind (the angle of attack). In a good breeze, a kite's weight is very small compared to the forces of lift and drag.

Drag
Air moving over and around the kite causes drag.

Weight
The kite's weight pulls it down toward the earth.

Pull on tether
The tether holds the kite at an angle to the wind.

Flat kite

The oldest and simplest kite is the plane surface, or flat, kite. It has a simple diamond shape and a flat frame. Kites like these have been flown for thousands of years. Flat kites look very impressive strung together to make a spectacular, writhing pattern in the sky.

FACT BOX

• The first kites were made in China over 3,000 years ago. Seven hundred years ago, kites were being used to lift people into the sky to spy on enemy armies.

• In 1901, the first radio message was sent across the Atlantic Ocean. It was received by a 360-foot aerial held up by a kite.

• Some kites carry weather forecasting instruments nearly 5 miles high—almost as high as the world's tallest mountain, Everest.

Box kite

A square-shaped box kite is more complicated to make than a flat kite, but it is more stable and has better lift. It does not need a tail to keep it upright. Box kites can be a combination of triangles and rectangles. Large box kites have even been used to lift people off the ground.

Parasail

A parasail is a kite that can lift a person into the air. It does not rely on the wind, but instead, is towed behind a boat or a car. A parasail looks like a parachute that has been divided into different parts, called *cells*. Each cell can work independently from the others, catching as much wind as possible and providing more lift. Parasails usually fly about 150 feet above the ground.

MAKE A KITE

For 3,000 years, people have been making and flying kites. The first kites were made from cloth or paper attached to a light bamboo frame. As time went by, the simple secret of building a good kite was discovered—make it as light as possible for its size. Some kites can fly in very gentle breezes. Their surfaces are wide so that the breeze has a large area to push against. Their low weight means that a small amount of lift is enough to make them take off into the sky. The kite design shown in this project has been used for many hundreds of years. Try flying it in a steady wind. You might have to experiment with the position of the bridle and the length of the tail.

This kite's long tail will help to keep it upright and stop it from spinning around.

MATERIALS

You will need: two pieces of balsa wood (one about twice as long as the other), ruler, pen, string, scissors, tape, sheet of thin fabric or plastic, fabric glue, colored paper.

Make a kite

1 To make the frame, mark the center of the short piece of balsa and one-third of the way down the long piece. Tie the balsa together at the marks with string.

2 Run string between the points of the diamond; tape the string at the end of each piece of balsa and secure it at the top.

3 Lay the frame on top of the sheet of material or plastic. Cut all around it, 1½ inches away from the edge. This will give you enough to fold over the string outline.

4 Fold each edge of the material over the frame and stick the edges down firmly with fabric glue (or tape, if you are making the kite from plastic). Let the glue dry.

5 Tie a piece of string to the long wood, as shown—this is called the bridle. Tie the end of the ball of string to the middle of the bridle to make the tether.

6 To make the tail, fold sheets of colored paper accordion-style. Tie them at about 10-inch intervals along a piece of string that is about twice as long as the kite. Glue or tie the tail to the bottom tip of the kite.

This kite has been made to look like a face with a long trailing mustache. Highly decorative designs can make the simplest kite look very special. Have fun experimenting with the basic kite design shown in this project.

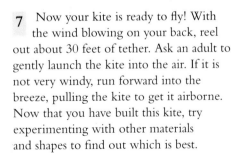

7 Now your kite is ready to fly! With the wind blowing on your back, reel out about 30 feet of tether. Ask an adult to gently launch the kite into the air. If it is not very windy, run forward into the breeze, pulling the kite to get it airborne. Now that you have built this kite, try experimenting with other materials and shapes to find out which is best.

LIGHTER THAN AIR

OIL floats on water because it is lighter than water. We say that oil is *less dense* than water. This means that a bottle full of oil weighs less than the same bottle filled with water. Water pushes upward on the oil with a force called *upthrust*. Watch smoke rising from a fire. Hot air is less dense than the cold air around it. The hot air floats upward, taking the smoke with it. A hot-air balloon is simply a huge bag full of hot air. It experiences upthrust from the cold air around it. The balloon takes off because the upthrust is greater than its own weight pulling it down. Like balloons, airships are lighter than the air around them. Modern airships are filled with a gas called *helium*, which is seven times lighter than air. Hot-air balloons and airships fly because the air around them pushes them upward, just like oil floating on water.

A candle heats the air around it. Snuff out the flame and the smoke is carried upward by the rising hot air.

Oil and water
Oil floats on water because it is less dense than water. The water surrounding the oil pushes upward on it. This push is called *upthrust*.

FACT BOX
• The very first balloon passengers were a sheep, a duck and a bird. They were sent up to make sure it was safe for people to travel by this new form of transport.

• The first balloon flight took place over Paris on November 21, 1783. It lasted 25 minutes.

• The first airship flight took place in France in 1852. Engineer Henri Giffard steered his steam-driven craft for about 18 miles at an average speed of just 5 miles per hour.

• At 750 feet long, the world's largest airship was the German *Hindenburg*. In 1937 it was destroyed when it burst into flames on landing, killing 35 people.

The first aviators

In 1783, brothers Joseph and Jacques Montgolfier built an enormous paper balloon and lit a fire underneath it. The balloon sailed into the sky, safely carrying two people into the air for the very first journey by hot-air balloon.

Hot-air balloons

Modern hot-air balloons are twice as tall as a house. They are made of nylon and can carry about five people in a basket hanging underneath. All hot-air balloons can go only where the wind blows them.

Modern airship

This airship uses helium to float. Unlike a hot-air balloon, it has engines and propellers to drive it along. The pilot steers by moving fins on the tail.

Airships in the 1930s were huge. They were filled with hydrogen gas that easily burst into flames, making the airships very dangerous.

MAKE A HOT-AIR BALLOON

Hot-air balloons rise into the sky because the hot air inside them is lighter than the cold air outside. The main part of the balloon is called the *envelope*. Hot air rises into the envelope from gas burners. The envelope fills with about 2½ tons of hot air (the same as the weight of two cars). This amount of hot air pushes cold air around the balloon out of the way. The weight of the cold air is about 3½ tons. The result is about 1 ton of upthrust, enough to lift the balloon, its passengers and tanks of gas off the ground. You can make and fly a model hot-air balloon to see it rise in exactly the same way.

M A T E R I A L S

You will need:
pencil, cardboard, ruler, scissors, sheets of tissue paper, glue stick, hair dryer.

Stabilize a balloon
Try adding modeling clay to the string of a helium balloon until the balloon hangs steady. The force downward (weight) now equals the force upward (upthrust).

Gas burners
Roaring gas burners heat the air inside the balloon. It takes more than half an hour to fill the balloon's envelope. When the envelope is full, the balloon is launched by untying ropes that hold it to the ground.

Make a hot-air balloon

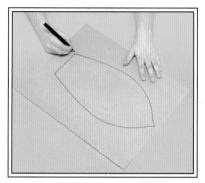

1 Draw a petal-shaped template on cardboard and cut it out. The shape should be 12 inches long and 5 inches across, with a flat bottom.

2 Draw around your template onto seven pieces of tissue paper. Be careful not to rip the paper with the tip of your pencil.

3 Carefully cut out the shapes you have drawn. You should now have seven petals that are all the same size and shape.

4 Glue along one edge of a petal. Lay another petal on top and press down. Open out and stick on another petal in the same way. Keep going until the balloon is complete.

5 To make your balloon fly, hold its neck open and fill the inside with hot air from a hair dryer. After ten seconds, switch off the hair dryer and let go of your balloon to launch it into the air.

Barb

Every feather has a hollow tube running down its center. Microscopic hooks lock each barb together so that air cannot pass through the feather.

BIRDS IN FLIGHT

MUSCLE-POWERED flight is very hard work. Although we have tried, no human has ever flown by flapping artificial wings. Compared to us, birds are light and very powerful. They are perfectly designed to stay up in the air. Birds' wings are covered in feathers— one of the strongest and lightest natural materials known. Their wings have an airfoil shape to provide lift, while their tail feathers help with steering and braking. Birds flap their wings hard to take off and climb into the air. A bird needs enormous flight muscles to provide enough power for flight—they can account for up to half the weight of a bird. These muscles are supplied by blood that is pumped by a large heart beating very fast. For humans to fly, we would need a chest the size of a barrel, arms 9 feet long, legs like broom handles and a head the size of an apple—as well as thousands of feathers!

Primary feathers

Flying feathers
The large primary flight feathers on the end of each wing produce most of the power for flight. These feathers can also be closed together or spread apart to control flight. Smaller secondary flight feathers on the inner wing form the curve that provides lift. The innermost feathers shape the wing into the bird's body and help to prevent turbulence in flight.

Secondary feathers

Flight feathers

Wing bone

Flight muscles

Breastbone

A bird's body

Flight feathers are connected to thin bones at the end of each wing. Bird bones are light—most are hollow and filled with air. The large flight muscles are anchored to the breastbone at the front of a bird's chest.

On the wing

This owl shows how a bird flies through the air. A bird's wings bend in the middle as they rise upward. The feathers open to help the air pass through the wings. On the powerful downstroke, the primary flight feathers slice through the air, pushing the air down and back and pulling the bird upward and forward.

FACT BOX

• A sparrow's heart beats 800 times a minute. When working very hard yours beats only about 120 times a minute.

• Birds are the only animals covered in feathers. A large bird, such as a swan, has about 25,000 feathers, while a tiny hummingbird has only 1,000.

• Arctic terns migrate each year from the Arctic to the Antarctic and back again—a round trip of about 6,000 miles.

• The world's largest bird, the ostrich, is simply too heavy to fly. The world's largest flying bird is the Australian Kori bustard, which weighs no more than 40 pounds.

Peregrine falcons are the fastest animals in the world. Folding back their wings to reduce drag, they dive at their prey at 210 miles per hour. The force of the impact breaks the victim's neck.

HOW BIRDS FLY

LOOK at a large bird, such as a goose, flying in the sky. Can you describe how its wings are moving? Flying birds do not simply flap their wings up and down. Their wings are not stiff and flat—instead, each wing has a joint like an elbow in the middle. This joint allows the wing to bend on the upstroke and flatten on the downstroke. Birds also open and close their flight feathers. On the upstroke, the feathers are separated so that air can pass easily through the wings. On the downstroke, the feathers are held together so that they provide the maximum amount of lift.

Start the project on these pages with a simple water test to feel how a bird's primary flight feathers work. You can then go on to build a model bird to see how birds move their wings in flight.

When a bird raises its wings (the upstroke), its feathers open to allow the air through. Feel the effect by moving your hand through water with your fingers spread open.

During the downstroke, a bird closes its flight feathers so its wings push hard against the air. This pushes the bird up and forward. Now close your fingers and move your hand through the water. Can you feel a difference?

Make a model bird

1 Start by making the bird's legs. Fold a piece of paper in half lengthwise several times until it is about 1 inch across.

2 Fold the strip in half and make a fold at each end to make the feet. Tape the feet to your work surface to keep your model stable.

3 To make the body, roll a piece of paper into a tube and secure the edge with tape. Use more tape to stick the body to the legs.

4 To make the wings, fold a piece of paper twice lengthwise so that it is about six times longer than it is wide. Fold it into a W shape.

5 Stick the wings onto the body. You have now made a model bird. To mimic how a bird flies, hold one wing tip in each hand.

6 Move your hands in circles— one going clockwise, the other counterclockwise. At takeoff, a bird's wings make large, round circles.

MATERIALS

You will need: sheets of paper, tape, scissors, glue stick.

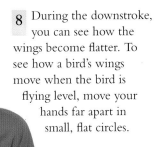

8 During the downstroke, you can see how the wings become flatter. To see how a bird's wings move when the bird is flying level, move your hands far apart in small, flat circles.

7 During the upstroke, notice how the wings bend in the middle. Some birds even bang their wings together at the top of the upstroke.

INSECT WINGS

Like all insects, a dragonfly's wings are thin and light. They are strengthened by a network of hollow tubes, called veins.

Dragonfly darter

Insects' wings and birds' wings work in completely different ways. Insects' wings are flat and stiff. They do not have an airfoil shape, but instead churn up the air to make swirling currents that provide lift. Forward movement is due to the wings pushing backward as they beat downward. Flying insects can hover and then dart off in any direction, twisting and turning through the air. They can even fly backward. Insects control their flight by beating their wings in extremely complicated patterns. Unlike most birds, the upstroke is as powerful as the downstroke. Many flying insects, such as bees, wasps and moths, have two pairs of wings, but some, such as flies and mosquitoes, have only one.

One of the most skilled flying insects is the dragonfly. Most insects flap their wings together, but a dragonfly uses its two pairs of wings separately.

As it beats its front wings down, a whirlwind is stirred up. This passes over the back wings, generating lift. A segmented tail helps the dragonfly steer.

With each beat, the wings push air down and back, moving the dragonfly up and forward. Its wings bend as they flap, giving more control during flight.

Butterflies

Butterflies have
two pairs of wings that
are hooked together so they act like one. Many
butterflies have square-shaped wings that flap
quite slowly. Their wings are covered with
powdery colored scales. The largest butterflies
have wingspans up to 10 inches across.

Beetle wings

A beetle's front wings are hard covers that are used to protect
the flying wings underneath. In flight, the wing covers stick
out, helping to steady the beetle's body.

FACT BOX

• Insects beat their wings at different speeds.
The wings of a large dragonfly beat 35 times a
second, a housefly, 200 times a second and a
mosquito, 600 times a second. The faster the
wings beat, the higher the buzzing sound.

• The record speed for an insect is held by a
dragonfly at 55 miles per hour. A housefly
can reach 3½ miles per hour and a mosquito
¾ mile per hour.

• Monarch butterflies migrate more than
1,000 miles across North America each year.

• For its size, a dragonfly generates three
times the lift of the most efficient aircraft.

*Flight
muscles*

Insect bodies

The body of this fly is
like a hard box with all
the soft parts inside. The
wings are attached to the
thorax, the central part of the
insect's body. Hinged
joints allow each wing
to move in any direction.
Large muscles inside pull on
the thorax, moving the
wings up and down.

AMAZING FLYING ANIMALS

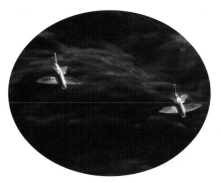

Flying fish swim very fast, close to the surface of the water. With wing-shaped fins stretched out, they leap upward and forward into the air, thrashing the water with their tails until they reach takeoff.

THE only animals that can fly, apart from birds and insects, are bats. Bats have wings that can push downward to create lift. Unlike birds, most bats are nocturnal—they sleep in the day and fly at night. A few other kinds of animals can fly through the air, but they cannot control or power their flight with flapping wings. Instead, they glide down through the air in search of food, or to escape from their enemies. These animals include flying frogs, flying lizards and flying squirrels. They jump outward from high places, moving forward through the air as they parachute downward. Flying fish sail along through the air using two fins that look like wings. Their gliding flight lasts only a few seconds, but they glide much faster than they can swim underwater.

FACT BOX

• Some flying fish can glide along at 30 miles per hour for several hundred yards. The record flight for a flying fish lasted 90 seconds and covered more than ½ mile.

• Flying foxes are actually a type of large fruit-eating bat. There are more than 2,000 species of bat living in the world.

• Flying snakes are able to flatten their bodies to help them glide from tree to tree.

• Some flying frogs jump from a height of 120 feet. They glide along, covering about 90 feet in only 8 seconds.

• The colugo, or flying lemur, can easily glide 300 feet or more between trees.

Flying frog
Flying frogs have enormous webbed feet. They use their feet as parachutes when they jump down from trees in search of insects. Altering the shape of their feet allows them to control their flight. Flying frogs have sticky pads on their toes to help them climb. Using these pads, they can cling to the smoothest leaves and branches in the rainforest.

Flying lizard
A flying lizard has flaps of skin along each side
of its body. These are supported by spines
hinged to the ribs. When danger threatens, the
spines stick out and the lizard glides away.

**Flying
squirrel**
Flying squirrels have folds of thin skin between their
front and rear legs. They glide from tree to tree by
stretching out their legs to spread the skin wide.

Bat wings
A bat's wing is a sheet
of flexible skin stretched
between its fingers, the side
of its body and the back of its
legs. Bats can alter the shape of
their wings much more than birds can. They can
twist and turn like acrobats in the air as they chase
insects for food. The largest bats have wingspans up
to 6 feet, but weigh just over 2 pounds.

PREHISTORIC FLYERS

THE earliest known flying creature is the dragonfly. The first ones lived about 350 million years ago, during a hot swampy time called the *Carboniferous Period*. Many other flying insects evolved during the following 150 million years, many of them similar to the insects we know today. About 200 million years ago, the first gliding reptiles appeared. From them evolved pterosaurs, giant winged lizards, some with wingspans up to 36 feet across. Over 150 million years ago, the first feathered creature, *Archaeopteryx*, lived on earth. Scientists think it evolved from small dinosaurs and may be the first known bird.

This insect lived about 50 million years ago. It was caught in sticky tree resin. The resin gradually fossilized and changed into amber.

FACT BOX

• Some prehistoric dragonflies had wingspans of up to three feet across.

• The very first humans lived no earlier than one million years ago. Modern-looking birds have existed for over 30 million years.

• Modern birds have just two finger bones in each wing. *Archaeopteryx* had all five, complete with claws at the ends.

• Fish fossils are often found near pterosaurs, so these flying lizards may have lived at sea.

• The largest flying animal ever to have existed was a pterosaur called *Quetzalocoatlus*. It had a human-sized body and a wingspan of 36 feet—wider than a hang glider.

Gliding reptiles

The first flying reptiles were gliders. *Longisquama* had tall crests along its back that might have opened up like wings and helped it to glide. It probably searched for insects to eat.

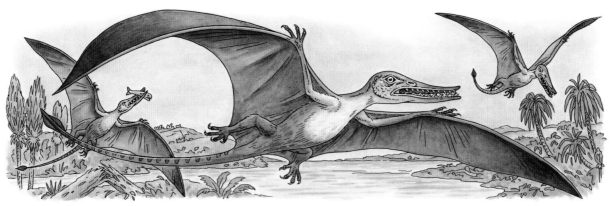

Giant pterosaurs

The first true flying reptiles were the pterosaurs. They lived at the same time as the dinosaurs and could reach huge sizes. Their wings were made of skin and their bodies were usually furry. They had light, delicate bones that reduced their weight and helped them fly.

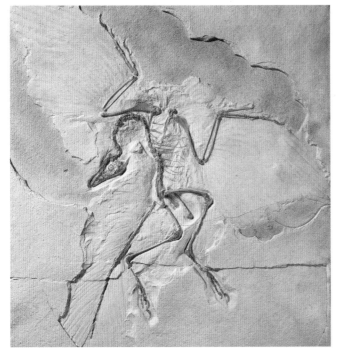

Archaeopteryx

Archaeopteryx had birdlike wings and legs, but a mouth full of teeth and a tail like a lizard. It was thickly feathered, but many scientists do not think it could fly very well. The first *Archaeopteryx* fossil was found in a quarry in Germany in 1860. Since then, six more have been discovered.

Fossilized feathers

This is a fossilized skeleton of an *Archaeopteryx*. When the animal died, all the skin and flesh rotted away. Buried deep underground, the skeleton slowly turned to stone.

AIRCRAFT WINGS

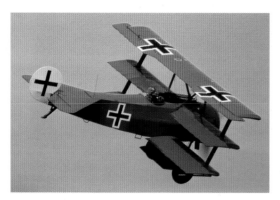

This aircraft is called a triplane *because it has three sets of wings. Early planes needed more sets of wings to provide enough lift, because they were slow.*

THE smallest microlight carries one person and weighs less than 200 pounds. The largest passenger jet carries over 500 people and weighs nearly 400 tons. But whatever the size or shape, all airplanes have one thing in common—they all have wings. Wings provide the lift aircraft need to hold them up in the air. The shape of the wings depends on how fast and high an aircraft must fly. Swept-back wings are needed for high-speed flight. Broad wings with a large area are needed to carry heavy loads. All wings have moving parts to help the aircraft land, take off and change direction.

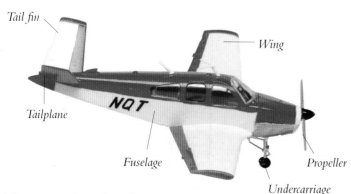

Tail fin

Wing

Tailplane

Fuselage

Propeller

Undercarriage

The parts of an aircraft

This picture shows the main parts of a small aircraft. They are needed for the aircraft to take off, fly level, change direction and land. The body of the aircraft is called the *fuselage* and the landing wheels are called the *undercarriage*. On many aircraft, the undercarriage folds up inside the body of the aircraft during flight to reduce drag. Hinged control surfaces on the tail and the wings are used to steer the aircraft from left to right, as well as up and down.

Piper Cadet

Like most airplanes, this small aircraft is called a *monoplane* because it has one set of wings. The wings stick straight out from the aircraft's body because it flies fairly slowly. This arrangement provides the greatest lift.

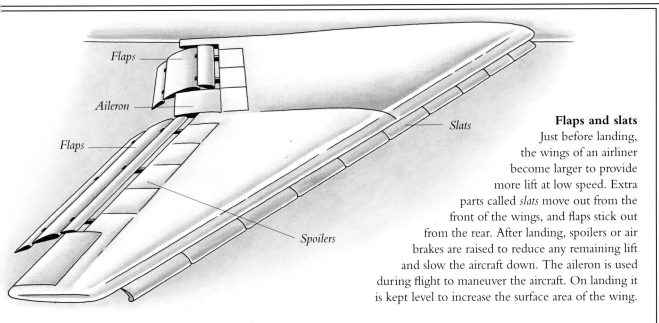

Flaps

Aileron

Flaps

Slats

Spoilers

Flaps and slats

Just before landing, the wings of an airliner become larger to provide more lift at low speed. Extra parts called *slats* move out from the front of the wings, and flaps stick out from the rear. After landing, spoilers or air brakes are raised to reduce any remaining lift and slow the aircraft down. The aileron is used during flight to maneuver the aircraft. On landing it is kept level to increase the surface area of the wing.

Boeing 747

Wide-bodied jets, like this Boeing 747, fly high and fast. Large wings provide enough lift to carry nearly 400 tons. The wings are tapered and swept back to keep drag low when flying at 600 miles per hour. Swept-back wings reduce lift, so a high takeoff speed is needed.

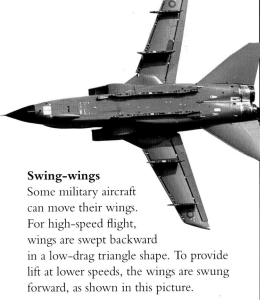

Swing-wings

Some military aircraft can move their wings. For high-speed flight, wings are swept backward in a low-drag triangle shape. To provide lift at lower speeds, the wings are swung forward, as shown in this picture.

FLYING AN AIRPLANE

Biplanes have two sets of wings. They are strong, agile and easy to fly and are often used as trainer planes or in acrobatic displays. Biplanes with open cockpits and wings braced with wires and struts were the most common airplane design until the 1930s.

To make a car turn left or right, all you have to do is turn the steering wheel. To steer a plane, you must move two sets of controls—one with your hands and one with your feet. Moving these controls alters the control surfaces on the plane's wings and tail. Control surfaces are small hinged flaps that affect how air flows around the plane. There are three main types of control surface: the ailerons attached to the rear edge of each wing, the elevators mounted at the rear of the tailplane, and the rudder at the rear of the tail fin. The pilot can also control flight by engine power—more power increases speed and so increases lift. So, an accelerating aircraft flying level will steadily gain height.

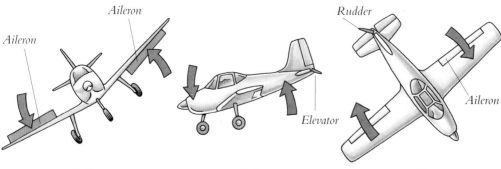

Roll

The ailerons on an aircraft operate in opposite directions from each other. When one aileron is raised, the other is lowered. The wing with the lowered aileron rises while the wing with the raised aileron drops.

Pitch

The elevators on the plane's tail are raised or lowered to make the plane's nose rise or fall. Lowering the elevators causes the aircraft's nose to drop, putting the plane into a dive. Raising the elevators causes the aircraft to climb.

Yaw

When the rudder is swiveled to one side, the aircraft moves left or right. Whichever way the rudder points, the aircraft's nose is deflected in the same direction. The rudder is used together with the ailerons to make a turn.

Control surfaces

To turn the aircraft (*yaw*), the pilot turns the rudder to one side. To make the aircraft descend or climb (*pitch*), the pilot adjusts the elevators on the tailplane. To roll (*tilt* or *bank*) the aircraft to the right or left, the ailerons are raised on one wing and lowered on the other.

Turning

When an aircraft turns, it moves quite a bit like a cyclist going around a corner. It banks as it turns, which means that it leans to one side with one wing higher than the other. This means that some of the lift from the wings is used to turn the aircraft and help it turn smoothly.

Inside the cockpit of a modern small aircraft, the pilot moves throttle levers to control engine power. The control column and pedals move the control surfaces. Dials and gauges show such things as fuel consumption, flight direction, altitude and how level the plane is flying.

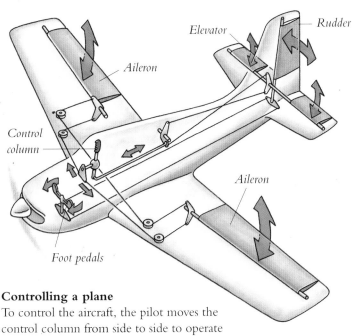

Elevator

Rudder

Aileron

Control column

Aileron

Foot pedals

Controlling a plane

To control the aircraft, the pilot moves the control column from side to side to operate the ailerons. Moving the control column back or forward operates the elevators. The foot pedals move the rudder from side to side.

FACT BOX

• Many flight terms are borrowed from terms used on board ships, for example rudder, *port* (left) and *starboard* (right).

• It takes an airliner one minute and just over 1 mile of airspace to reverse its course.

• A cruising airliner loses 3 tons in weight per hour as fuel is used up.

• Many aircraft use computer-controlled autopilot systems. These automatically set the controls for takeoff and landing.

• To control a helicopter, the angle of the rotor blades is adjusted. This allows the pilot to hover, go straight upward, forward, backward and even sideways.

MAKE A MODEL PLANE

T HE previous two pages explained how the control surfaces on the wings and the tail of an aircraft work—they change the way air flows over the aircraft, allowing the pilot to steer the aircraft in different directions. Working together, the ailerons and rudder make the plane turn to the left or right. Moving the elevators on the tail makes the nose of the plane go up or down. This project shows you how to make a model plane, allowing you to see for yourself how the control surfaces work. Although a model is much smaller than a real full-size aircraft, it flies in exactly the same way. The scientific rules of flying are the same for any aircraft, from an airliner weighing 350 tons to this simple model made from pieces of paper and a drinking straw and stuck together with tape.

M A T E R I A L S

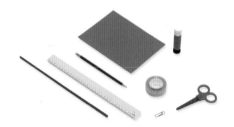

You will need:
pencil, ruler, paper, scissors, glue,
tape, drinking straw, paper clip.

Make a model plane

1 Cut two paper rectangles, one 10 inches by 4 inches, the other 9 by 2 inches. Mark two 2½-inch ailerons on the larger, and elevators and the center line on the smaller.

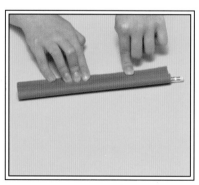

2 To make the wings, fold the larger rectangle over a pencil. Stick the top edge along the line you have drawn for the ailerons. Make cuts to allow the ailerons to move.

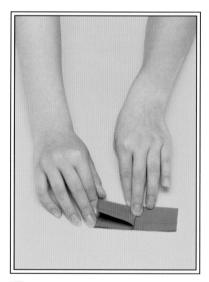

3 Fold the smaller rectangle in half and in half again to make a W. Stick its center together to make the upright fin. Make cuts to allow the rudder and elevators to move.

4 Use tape to stick the wings and tail to the straw (the plane's fuselage or body). Position the wings about three-quarters of the way along the fuselage.

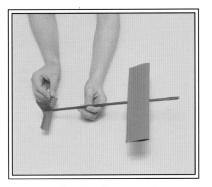

5 Try adjusting the control surfaces. Bend the elevators on the tail slightly up. This will make the plane climb as it flies. Bend the elevators down to make it dive.

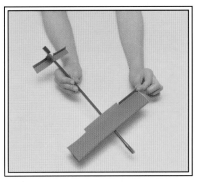

6 Bend the left-hand aileron up and the right-hand aileron down the same amount. Bend the rudder to the left. This will make the plane turn to the left as it flies.

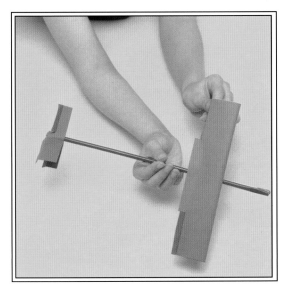

7 Bend the right-hand aileron up and the left-hand aileron down. Bend the rudder slightly to the right and the plane will turn to the right. Can you make it fly in a circle?

8 Launch your plane by throwing it steadily straight ahead. To make it fly well, use a paper clip or modeling clay to weight the nose.

PROPELLERS

ALL aircraft need thrust to push them through the air. A propeller whirling at high speed converts the power of an aircraft's engine into thrust. Propellers have two or more blades, each shaped like a long thin airfoil wing. The blades generate lift in a forward direction as they move through the air. Modern propellers have variable-pitch blades, which allow the pilot to alter the angle that the blades bite into the air. Changing the pitch of a propeller is like changing gears on a bicycle. For takeoff, the blades face forward and the engine spins very fast to generate maximum thrust. Less thrust is needed when cruising. To cruise, the blades are set at a sharper angle and the engine spins more slowly. This arrangement uses fuel most economically.

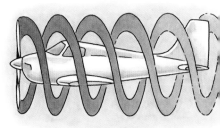

Propellers screw their way through the air in the same way a screw goes into wood. For this reason, aircraft driven by propellers are often known as airscrews. As the propeller turns, the blades strike the air and push it backward. This produces thrust and moves the aircraft forward.

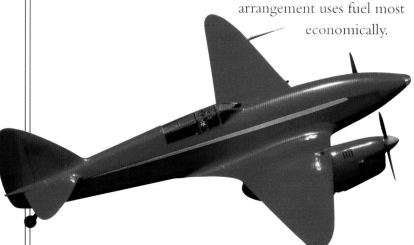

The DH-88 Comet
The DeHavilland DH-88 Comet took part in a race from England to Australia in 1934. It is shown here after it was restored for the fiftieth anniversary of the race. Each of its propellers is driven by its own engine. They are like huge car engines and are fueled by gasoline.

Wooden propellers
The first airplanes had propellers made from layers of wood glued together. The pilot would spin the propeller by hand to start the engine—a dangerous job, since the pilot could be hit.

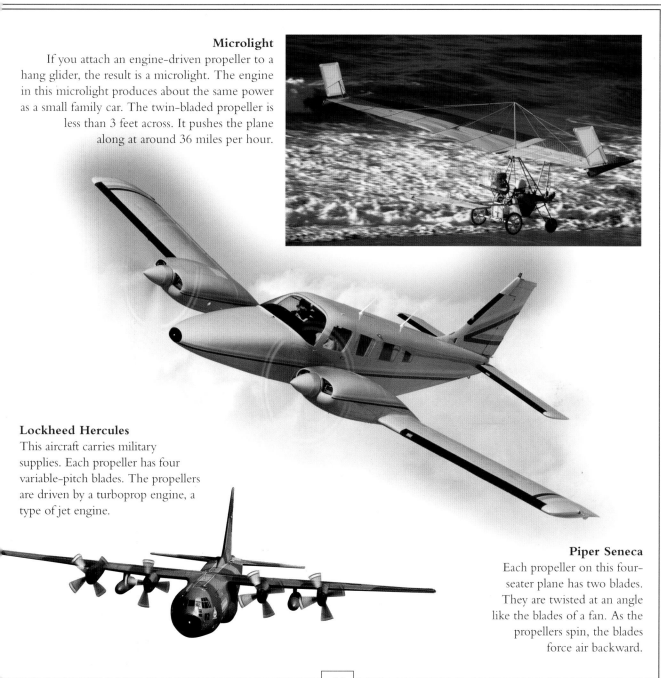

Microlight

If you attach an engine-driven propeller to a hang glider, the result is a microlight. The engine in this microlight produces about the same power as a small family car. The twin-bladed propeller is less than 3 feet across. It pushes the plane along at around 36 miles per hour.

Lockheed Hercules

This aircraft carries military supplies. Each propeller has four variable-pitch blades. The propellers are driven by a turboprop engine, a type of jet engine.

Piper Seneca

Each propeller on this four-seater plane has two blades. They are twisted at an angle like the blades of a fan. As the propellers spin, the blades force air backward.

MAKE A PROPELLER

MATERIALS

You will need:
thin paper, pencil, ruler,
scissors, paper clip.

A PROPELLER works in two different ways all at the same time, each complementing the other. When a propeller spins, it makes air move past it. Propeller-driven aircraft use this effect to produce thrust. Also, when air moves past a propeller, it makes the propeller spin. These projects look at propellers working in these two different ways. In the first, you can make a simple paper propeller called a *spinner*. As the spinner falls, moving air rushes past the blades, making it revolve. In the second project, you can make a spinning propeller fly upward through the air. The propeller blades are set at an angle, like the blades of a fan. They whirl around and make air move. The moving air produces thrust and lifts the propeller upward.

Children first flew propellers like this 600 years ago in China.

Make a spinner

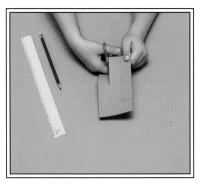

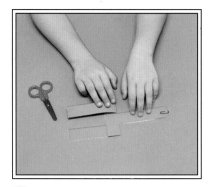

1 Take a piece of paper, about 6 inches by 4 inches, and draw a T-shape on it as shown in the picture above. With a pair of scissors, cut along the two long lines of the T.

2 Fold along the two short lines to make two wings and a stalk, as shown above. Attach a paper clip to the bottom. Open the wings flat to make two blades. Now drop the spinner. What happens?

Before dropping it again, try giving each blade a twist to make your spinner spin around faster.

Make a propeller

1 With a compass, draw a circle about 4 inches across on the cardboard. Draw a circle 1 inch across in the center. With the protractor, draw lines dividing it into 16 equal sections.

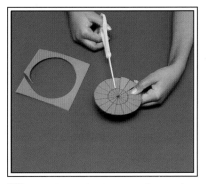

2 Cut along the lines to the circle in the center. Twist the blades up and down a little to angle them.

M A T E R I A L S

You will need: thick cardboard, ruler, compass, protractor, pen, scissors, ½-inch slice of cork, awl, dowel, model glue, string, thread spool.

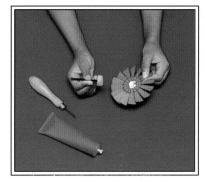

3 Make a hole in the center of the cork slice with the awl. Put glue on the end of the dowel and push it into the hole. Stick the cork in the middle of the propeller.

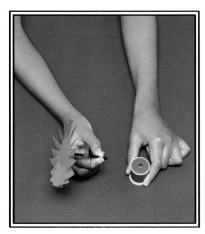

4 When the glue has dried, wind a long piece of string around the dowel. Drop the dowel into the thread spool. You are now ready for a test flight.

5 Pull steadily on the string to whirl the propeller around. As the end of the string comes away, the blades produce enough thrust to lift the spinning propeller out of the launcher and into the air.

JET ENGINES

MOST large modern aircraft are driven by jet engines. Jet-propelled aircraft fly faster than propeller-driven ones. They can fly high where the air is thin and drag is less. Jet engines have huge fans inside that suck in air and compress it. Burning fuel produces a roaring jet of hot gases that blasts from the rear of the engine, producing thrust. Some fighter aircraft rely on turbojet engines. They are very powerful, but noisy, and use enormous amounts of fuel. Passenger jets use turbofan engines that have an extra-large fan at the front of the engine. This fan produces most of the thrust by forcing air around the engine so that it combines with the jet of exhaust gases at the rear.

An octopus uses jet propulsion to move fast. It sucks in water and squeezes it out through a small hole. The jet of water pushes it along.

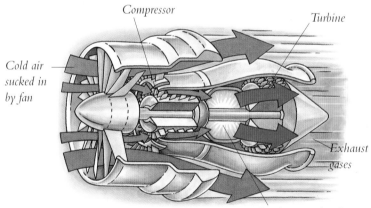

Compressor

Turbine

Cold air sucked in by fan

Exhaust gases

Combustion chamber

A turbofan engine
Jet engines are tube-shaped. Fast-spinning fans pull air into the jet engine. Fuel burns in the air and heats it. The exhaust gases spin the turbine that drives the compressor. Expanding gases leave the engine at over 6,000 feet per second. The blast of hot gases pushes the engine, and the aircraft, forward.

Inside a jet engine
This jet engine is shown with its protective casing removed for inspection. You can see the huge blades at the front that suck in air. Most of the small pipes supply fuel and lubricating oil to the parts inside.

The Blackbird
The Lockheed SR-71 Blackbird reconnaissance plane is powered by turbojet engines. In 1974, one flew from New York to London in 1 hour, 54 minutes —an unbroken record of 2,000 miles per hour. In the 1970s and 1980s, the US Air Force used these jet aircraft to fly at high altitudes and take aerial photographs of enemy territory.

Executive jet
Commuter jets like this one carry people on business trips. Its engines are on the tail, not on the wings, and can reach 480 miles per hour—nearly as fast as a large airliner.

Jumbo jet
The Boeing 747 was the very first of the wide-bodied jets. Introduced in 1970, it has made international jet travel commonplace.

Helicopter
This helicopter is powered by a turboshaft engine, a type of jet engine without a jet of gases. Most of the energy turns the rotors. Only a tiny bit helps to push the helicopter forward.

JETS AND TURBINES

THE previous pages explained how a jet engine produces thrust from a roaring jet of super-hot gas. The jet engine looks complicated, but the way it works is very simple. A jet moving in one direction produces thrust in the other direction. Imagine you are standing on a skateboard and squirting a powerful hose forward. Jet propulsion will push you backward. This reaction has been known about for nearly 2,000 years, but it was not until the 1930s that it was used in an engine.

In the first project, you can make a jet zoom along a string. The jet engine is a balloon that produces thrust from escaping air. The second project shows you how a set of blades, called a *turbine*, works. It uses hot air to turn the blades. When trying out this project, you must ask an adult to help you light the candles. These projects may seem very simple, but they use the same scientific principles that propel all jet airplanes through the air.

M A T E R I A L S

You will need:
long, thin balloon, drinking straw, tape, scissors, string.

Make a balloon jet

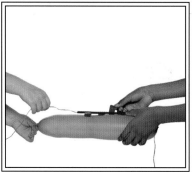

1 Blow up the balloon and, keeping a tight hold on the neck, tape the straw to the top of it. Now thread the string through the straw. Stretch the string level across the room.

2 Let go of the neck of the balloon. A stream of air jets backward and produces thrust. This propels the balloon forward along the string at high speed. Bring the balloon back, blow it up and try another flight.

Make a turbine

1 Use a pair of kitchen scissors to cut out the bottom of a large aluminum pie plate.

2 Mark a smaller circle and 16 equal sections in the same way as on page 43 and cut along each one.

3 Angle the blades by twisting them slightly up and down. You have now made your turbine.

MATERIALS

You will need: scissors, aluminum pie plate, compass, protractor, ruler, pin, dowel, sticky tape, bead, thread spool, modeling clay, plate, candles, matches.

6 Make a hole in the center of the turbine and place it on the pin. Ask an adult to light the candles. Hot air will spin the blades.

4 Tape the blunt end of the pin to one end of the dowel. Place the bead on the pin.

5 Put the dowel in the thread spool and press the spool into modeling clay in the center of the plate.

BREAKING THE SOUND BARRIER

THE sound barrier is like an invisible wall that travels in front of a speeding aircraft. Where does it come from? As an airplane flies, it sends out pressure waves through the air. These waves are like the ripples around a moving boat. The waves move away from the aircraft at the speed of sound. When the aircraft is traveling at the speed of sound, the waves cannot outrun it. They build up and compress the air in front of the aircraft. To fly faster than the speed of sound, the aircraft must fly through this barrier of dense air and overtake it. The aircraft goes through the sound barrier with a jolt because drag increases suddenly. Shock waves then spread out and can be heard on the ground as a rumbling sonic boom.

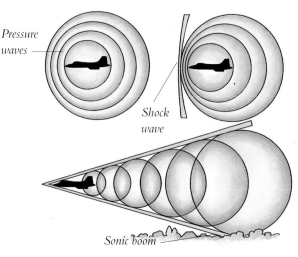

Pressure waves

Shock wave

Sonic boom

As an aircraft flies along, it sends out pressure waves. When the aircraft flies at the speed of sound, a shock wave builds up in front of it. As the aircraft accelerates through the sound barrier, the shock wave breaks away to be heard on the ground as a sonic boom.

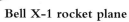

Bell X-1 rocket plane
In 1947, the rocket-powered Bell X-1 was the first aircraft to travel faster than the speed of sound (which is called *Mach 1*).

The Bell X-1 was dropped from a B29 bomber at 18,000 feet. As the pilot climbed to 39,000 feet, the aircraft broke through the sound barrier.

Pilot's-eye view

A large transparent canopy gives the pilot a good field of view. Fighter pilots need an array of computers in the cockpit to cope with the enormous amounts of information they need to fly their jets.

Jet fighter

The Mirage flies at more than twice the speed of sound. It climbs almost straight upward, speeding faster than a rifle bullet. It can reach the same height as a cruising airliner in about one minute. The Mirage is used by air forces around the world—different models can be used as fighters, fighter bombers and for reconnaissance.

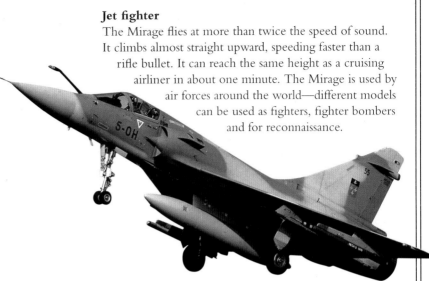

Concorde

The Concorde is the world's only supersonic passenger aircraft. It cruises at 1,300 miles per hour, over twice the speed of an ordinary airliner, and can cross the Atlantic Ocean in just over three hours. Its engines, however, are noisy and use a lot of fuel.

FACT BOX

• The speed of sound can change. It depends on air temperature and density. Sound travels faster in warm air. At sea level (68°F), Mach 1 is 735 miles per hour, but at 36,000 feet (12°F) Mach 1 is 636 miles per hour.

• Subsonic speeds are below Mach 0.8 (jumbo jets). Transonic speeds are between Mach 0.8 and Mach 1.2 (breaking the sound barrier). Supersonic speeds are between Mach 1.2 and Mach 5 (Concorde and fighter jets). Hypersonic speeds are above Mach 5 (the space shuttle during re-entry).

• The first supersonic civilian aircraft to fly was the Russian Tupolev Tu-144 on the last day of 1968, two months before the Concorde.

GOING UP

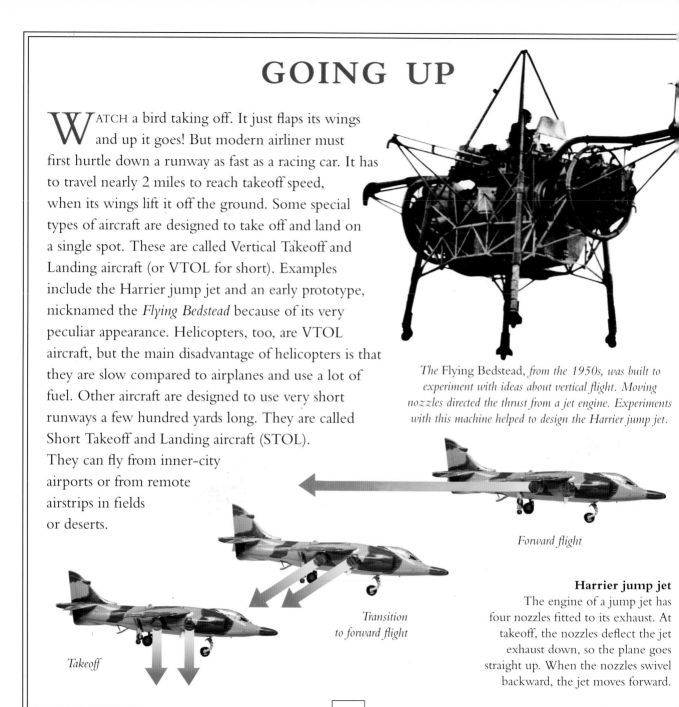

WATCH a bird taking off. It just flaps its wings and up it goes! But modern airliner must first hurtle down a runway as fast as a racing car. It has to travel nearly 2 miles to reach takeoff speed, when its wings lift it off the ground. Some special types of aircraft are designed to take off and land on a single spot. These are called Vertical Takeoff and Landing aircraft (or VTOL for short). Examples include the Harrier jump jet and an early prototype, nicknamed the *Flying Bedstead* because of its very peculiar appearance. Helicopters, too, are VTOL aircraft, but the main disadvantage of helicopters is that they are slow compared to airplanes and use a lot of fuel. Other aircraft are designed to use very short runways a few hundred yards long. They are called Short Takeoff and Landing aircraft (STOL). They can fly from inner-city airports or from remote airstrips in fields or deserts.

The Flying Bedstead, *from the 1950s, was built to experiment with ideas about vertical flight. Moving nozzles directed the thrust from a jet engine. Experiments with this machine helped to design the Harrier jump jet.*

Forward flight

Transition to forward flight

Takeoff

Harrier jump jet
The engine of a jump jet has four nozzles fitted to its exhaust. At takeoff, the nozzles deflect the jet exhaust down, so the plane goes straight up. When the nozzles swivel backward, the jet moves forward.

DeHavilland Dash
This aircraft is used on short runways in cities. It has four extraquiet engines and can carry up to 54 passengers. Its large wings provide plenty of lift and are set high on its body to keep the propellers clear off the ground. The Dash can take off on a runway just 2,100 feet long.

Autogyro
The autogyro is a cross between an airplane and a helicopter. The rotor is not driven by the engine. During flight, rushing air spins the rotor, which provides most of the lift to keep the autogyro up in the air.

Bell-Boeing Osprey
The Osprey is known as a tilt-rotor aircraft. The giant propellers are called proprotors. Mounted at the tips of the wings, they tilt upward for takeoff, like a helicopter. For forward flight, they swing into the propeller position of an airplane. The Osprey can fly about three times as far as a helicopter on the same fuel load.

STRANGE AIRCRAFT

M ANY aircraft have strange shapes. The Belluga looks like an enormous rotund dolphin with wings. The fabric used to make the wings of a pedal-powered aircraft is so thin, that light shines through it. In all cases, an aircraft's strange appearance is due to its special design for a particular purpose. The Belluga is designed to carry large items that will not fit into the cargo hold of an ordinary transport airplane. Pedal-powered aircraft must be ultralight, so their wings are covered in thin plastic film. The people who design new planes are called aeronautical engineers. They can design planes for all sorts of different purposes—to carry enormous loads, to fly superfast, or even to fly nonstop around the world. But no matter how strange an aircraft looks, it must be designed to take off, fly straight and level, and land safely.

The Optica observation plane was designed for low-speed flight and to give a clear view. It is used to observe such things as problems with traffic flow or crop growth.

Pedal power
Gossamer Albatross was the first pedal-powered aircraft. A strong man has less power than a lawn-mower engine, so the ultralight plane was made of thin plastic stretched on ribs only ½ inch thick.

World voyager
In 1986, *Voyager* took nine days to fly Americans Jeana Yeager and Dick Rutan nonstop around the world without refueling. Each wing of the specially built plane was four times the length of the fuselage, providing the greatest lift with the lowest drag.

Invisible fighter

The F-117 Stealth Fighter is made up of flat, slab-shaped panels and special materials. These scatter beams from enemy radars and make the plane almost undetectable. Ordinary planes reflect radar beams straight back so they can be spotted. The F-117's low, flat shape reflects radar waves in directions other than back to the receiver, while special paint absorbs some of the radar waves.

A whale of a plane

The Belluga transport plane can carry almost 25 tons of cargo in its 24-foot-high hold. The Belluga is enormous, but it has the streamlined shape of a dolphin to help reduce drag.

Solar power

Solar Challenger was the world's first solar-powered aircraft. At 125 pounds, it is still the lightest powered aircraft. Solar cells on the wings changed sunlight into electricity. An electric motor drove the propellers.

FACT BOX
- In 1907, one of the first British powered flights was made in a bizarre looking multiplane known as the *Venetian Blind*. It had nearly 50 sets of wings.

- The aircraft with the longest wingspan was a flying boat, the *Spruce Goose*. Designed by eccentric millionaire Howard Hughes, it had a wingspan of over 300 feet. It made its first and only flight in November 1947.

- Some large, propeller-driven planes are used to scoop up huge amounts of water from lakes. They then drop their load like a water bomb to put out forest fires.

FLYING THROUGH WATER

This boat is using hydrofoils to lift its hull completely out of the water. At rest, it floats on the water like a normal boat.

WINGS can also work underwater. Some boats have underwater wings, called *hydrofoils*. As the boat speeds along, the hydrofoils lift it upward, out of the water. The hull of the boat is then traveling in the air, so drag is greatly reduced. Hydrofoil boats can travel at 60 miles per hour, over three times as fast as an ordinary boat. Hovercraft virtually fly across the sea, just an inch or so above the water's surface. Powerful fans blow air down through a rubber skirt to provide a cushion of air. This cushion cuts down the friction between the hovercraft and the water below. Propellers drive the hovercraft forward at up to 72 miles per hour.

MATERIALS

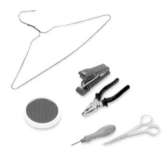

You will need: the lid of a margarine container, scissors, stapler, awl, pliers, coat hanger wire (ask an adult to cut out the bottom section).

How a hydrofoil works

1 Cut a rectangle of plastic, 2 inches by 4 inches, from the lid of the margarine container. Fold it in half to make a hydrofoil. Staple the ends ½ inch in from the back edge.

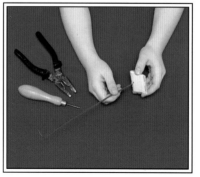

2 Use an awl to make two holes in the front of the hydrofoil, ½ inch from the front edge. Use pliers to bend one end of the wire. Slide the hydrofoil onto the wire.

3 Try moving your hydrofoil in air—it will not lift up. Pull it through water and it will rise up the wire.

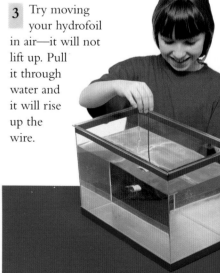

How a hovercraft works

1 Use a pencil to poke a hole through the middle of the polystyrene tray. The hole should be about ½ inch across.

2 Blow up the balloon with the pump and push its neck through the hole. Pinch the neck of the balloon to stop the air from escaping.

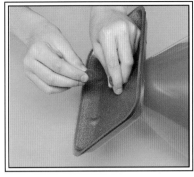

3 Keep pinching with one hand, using the other hand to slip the button into the neck. The button will control how fast the air escapes.

M A T E R I A L S

You will need: polystyrene tray, pencil, balloon, balloon pump, button.

4 Place the tray on a table. Air escapes steadily from under the tray's edges, lifting it slightly off the table. Give the tray a gentle push and it will skate along.

A hovercraft's rubber skirt is the black part just above the water. You can see how the air cushion makes the water spray around. Four large propellers drive the hovercraft in any direction.

ROCKETS AND SPACEFLIGHT

WHY can't an airplane fly off into space? The main reason is that there is no air in space. Air becomes thinner higher up. Wings need air to provide lift, so airplanes cannot fly above about 130,000 feet. Jets use oxygen from the air to burn fuel. There is not enough oxygen for them to work properly above about 65,000 feet. Rockets can work in space because they carry oxygen with them. There are two main types of rocket: liquid-fueled rockets and solid-fueled rockets. Liquid-fueled rockets carry liquid oxygen to burn their fuel (liquid hydrogen). Solid-fueled rockets are like enormous fireworks. They contain chemicals that release oxygen when heated.

Blast-off
The space shuttle has three liquid-fuel engines. They burn a mixture of liquid oxygen and liquid hydrogen from a strapped-on tank. Extra thrust comes from two solid-fuel booster rockets. The tank and boosters fall away when their fuel is used up.

Landing shuttle
The space shuttle takes off like a rocket, but lands like a glider. It glides down toward a runway just like an ordinary aircraft and deploys a parachute to help it roll to a stop. Each shuttle is expected to make 100 launches in its lifetime.

FACT BOX
- Liquid oxygen is stored at -297.4°F; liquid hydrogen at -427°F. By comparison, it is only -40°F at the South Pole.

- The engines of the space shuttle develop 2,200 tons of thrust at takeoff—20 times more than the engines of a jet airliner.

- To escape the earth's gravity, a rocket must reach a speed of about 7 miles per second. This is called the *escape velocity*. If a rocket does not reach this speed, gravity will pull it back.

- Solid-fuel rockets were invented in China nearly 1,000 years ago. They were fueled by gunpowder and were used to scare enemies.

Syncom

This communications satellite relays radio and TV signals all around the world. It was taken into space by the shuttle and it is held in orbit by the earth's gravity. It is traveling at a fast enough speed to prevent it falling back to earth.

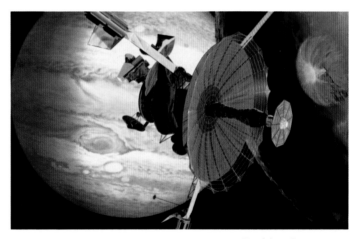

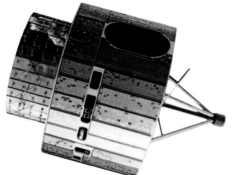

Meteosat

This weather satellite was carried into space by the shuttle, which only goes into a low earth orbit. A small rocket pushed the satellite 21,000 miles farther out. From this height, it can send back pictures of half the earth's surface.

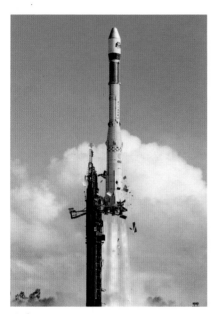

Ariane

A three-stage rocket, Ariane has three rockets mounted one above the other. After takeoff, the first stage falls away when its fuel is used up. The second stage then fires, followed by the third.

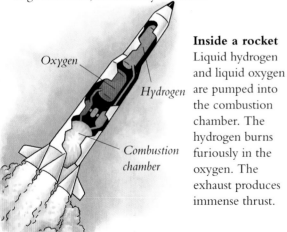

Oxygen

Hydrogen

Combustion chamber

Inside a rocket

Liquid hydrogen and liquid oxygen are pumped into the combustion chamber. The hydrogen burns furiously in the oxygen. The exhaust produces immense thrust.

Probing into space

This picture shows the space probe *Galileo* approaching the planet Jupiter in 1995. Launched by the shuttle, it used the gravity of the planets to acclerate itself toward its destination.

MAKE A ROCKET

Rockets have powerful engines used to carry satellites into orbit more than 200 miles above the earth's surface.

SPACE rockets rely on jet propulsion to fly. A stream of hot gases roars out from the tail end and the rocket surges forward. Deep under the sea, octopuses rely on jet propulsion to escape from their enemies. They squirt out a jet of water and shoot off in the opposite direction. This project shows you how to make and fly a rocket that uses jet propulsion. The thrust of a rocket depends on the mass of propellant it shoots out every second. Water is a much better propellant than hot gas, because it is so much heavier. Follow these instructions carefully and your rocket could fly more than 75 feet above the ground. You may need adult help to make some parts of this rocket and to launch it. When you are ready for a test flight, set your rocket up in an open space, well away from trees and buildings. This rocket is very powerful—do not stand over it while it is being launched. Wear clothes that you do not mind getting very wet!

Make a rocket

M A T E R I A L S

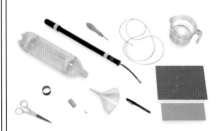

You will need:
pen, cardboard, colored cardboard, scissors, plastic bottle, tape, funnel, pitcher of water, awl, cork, air valve, plastic tubing, bicycle pump.

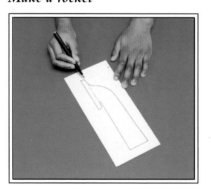

1 Rockets have fins to make them fly straight. Draw this fin template (it is about 8 inches long) onto plain cardboard and use it to cut out four fins from colored cardboard.

2 Decorate your bottle to look like a rocket. Fold over the tab at the top of each fin. Use long pieces of tape to firmly attach the fins to the bottle.

3 Use the funnel to half fill the bottle with water. (The water is the propellant. Compressed air above the water will provide the energy that makes the thrust.)

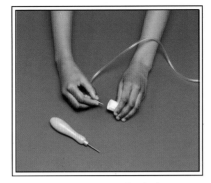

4 Use the awl to drill a hole through the cork. Push the wide end of the air valve into the plastic tubing. Push the valve through the hole in the cork.

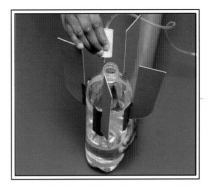

5 Push the cork and valve into the neck of the bottle. Make sure it is pushed in firmly so that the cork does not come out too easily.

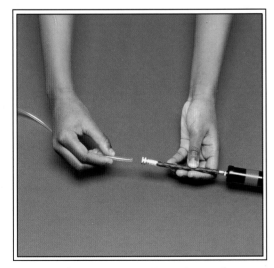

6 Attach the other end of the plastic tubing to the bicycle pump. Turn your rocket the right way up—you are now ready to launch your rocket outside. Look for a launch site well away from trees and buildings.

7 Stand the rocket on its tail fins. Start pumping. Bubbles of air will rise up through the water. When the pressure in the bottle gets high enough, the cork and water will be forced out and the rocket will fly upward.

THE HISTORY OF FLIGHT

SINCE ancient times, human beings have wished they could fly. The first people to get off the ground were the Chinese—they used kites to lift people into the air over 700 years ago. In the eighteenth century, lighter-than-air balloons carried their first passengers, and in 1852, the world's first airship flight occurred. But it was not until the invention of the petrol engine in the 1880s that true powered flight in a heavier-than-air machine became possible. In 1903, the Wright brothers made the world's first powered, controlled and sustained flight in their aircraft, *Flyer 1*.

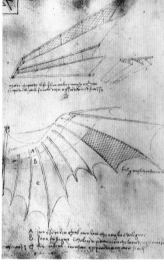

About 500 years ago, the Italian artist and inventor Leonardo da Vinci drew many designs for flying machines. His scientific ideas about flight were correct, but a human could not provide enough power to make them work.

Clément Ader
In 1890, Ader's steam-driven aircraft *Eole* became the first full-size airplane to leave the ground. It managed to hop 150 feet. It was not considered true powered flight because it was uncontrolled.

Otto Lilienthal
German experimenter Otto Lilienthal built hang gliders in the 1890s from reeds covered with shirt material. He made over 2,000 flights and showed how curved airfoil wings work better than flat ones. He was the first person to make repeated, controlled flights, but while making a test flight, Lilienthal crash-landed and died.

Orville and Wilbur Wright

On December 17, 1903, American inventor Orville Wright flew *Flyer 1* for 108 feet at a height of about 9 feet. This was the first time a human had made a controlled powered takeoff, flight and landing.

Louis Blériot

In 1909, Frenchman Louis Blériot became the first person to fly across the English Channel. At an average speed of 36 miles per hour it took him 37 minutes. He reported that he had to wrestle constantly with the controls to keep his monoplane flying steadily. The picture shows a modern replica of his plane.

Charles Lindberg

In 1927, American Charles Lindberg was the first person to fly alone and nonstop across the Atlantic Ocean in his tiny Ryan monoplane, *The Spirit of St. Louis*. He took 33 hours and 39 minutes to fly 3,600 miles from New York to Paris, flying at an average speed of 120 miles per hour.

FACT BOX

• 1908, Orville Wright made the first sustained, powered flight lasting one hour.

• 1937, the jet engine was designed by British engineer Frank Whittle.

• 1939, American engineer Igor Sikorsky designed the first modern helicopter.

• 1947, the first aircraft flew at supersonic speed in the United States.

• 1952, the first jet airliner, the DeHavilland Comet, entered service in England.

• 1970, Boeing 747 jumbo jet entered service.

• 1976, Concorde started transatlantic service.

FLIGHT INTO THE FUTURE

Birds have been flying for more than 30 million years. Humans first took to the air 200 years ago. Now the air is full of aircraft of all descriptions. You can fly halfway around the world in less than 24 hours. Some planes fly three times faster than sound. So what does the future hold? Look up into the sky in ten years' time and what will you see? Engineers are developing new and more powerful engines, new resin materials that are lighter and stronger than metal, and strange new wing shapes to help aircraft fly faster and higher. Whatever happens, human flight will increase—but at what cost to the health of our environment and the birds and animals who share it?

This Boeing 747-400 can carry up to 567 passengers. It is the latest double-decker version of the 1970s jumbo jet. Plans for a super-jumbo, the 747-600X, have been canceled due to cost.

Horizontal Takeoff and Landing (HOTOL)
This picture is an artist's impression of HOTOL riding piggy-back to 45,000 feet on the Antonin 225 (the world's largest airplane). It then uses rocket engines to fly into space. Traveling at Mach 5, it could fly from England to Australia in under four hours.

FACT BOX
• A Russian experimental plane, called the Aquatain, has been designed to gain extra lift by skimming across the surface of the ocean. The craft is reported to use much less fuel than a conventional aircraft.

• All new airplanes have to meet strict environmental rules governing noise levels and emissions that might further damage the sensitive ozone layer.

• Modern cockpits use advanced systems to reduce the pilot's workload. Holographic displays and keyboards project data onto a see-through screen, while optical fibers carry signals at the speed of light to the aircraft's control surfaces.

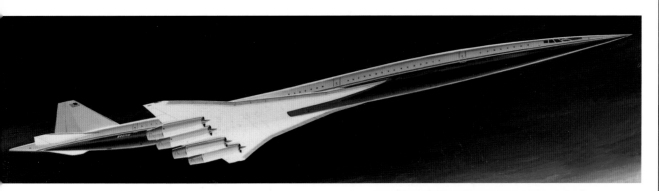

High Speed Civil Transport (HSCT)

Flying at Mach 3, this airliner may one day carry 200 passengers from New York to Tokyo in about three hours. Cruising above 54,000 feet, it will have low pollutant engines that will not damage the ozone layer.

X-30
space plane

Aircraft with rocket engines can travel extremely fast in space, because there is no air to create drag. This model shows what the X-30 space plane might look like, flying at up to Mach 5 through the edge of space to reach its destination.

X-29 experimental plane

The experimental X-29 aircraft refuels in midair from a tanker plane. The X-29 has unusual swept-forward wings. This gives high lift and low drag, making it very maneuverable. Tests with the X-29 may lead to new designs for passenger planes.

INDEX